I am LEARNING
HOW TO LISTEN TO MY BODY

WRITTEN AND ILLUSTRATED BY
SARAH WEISSMAN SELZNICK

ISBN 979-8-9896289-0-2

Visit the Author's website at www.sensoryexplorers.com

To Lilah

The world is busy and filled with noises, sights, sounds, and smells from *everything* around us.

Inside the classroom, our teacher says, "Circle time!" We pick our spots, and our teacher asks, "What do you hear?"

"A CLOCK!"
"The street!"
"My feet on the rug!"

"Very good!" our teacher says with a smile. "Now, let's take a deep breath and listen to what your body says to you."

"Huh?" I wonder. "What does that mean? The only part of my body that speaks is my mouth!"

Our teacher smiles again. "Our bodies speak to us in many different ways, and it's our job to listen and learn."

We all take a deep breath together. In… and out…

All of a sudden, I hear something! A grumble, rumble, and tumble!

I listen harder, and it gets louder… gurgle… flurgle…

I glance at the schedule and realize lunch is next.

"MY BODY IS TELLING ME IT'S HUNGRY!" I shout.

"How do you know?" teacher asks.

"I heard a rumble in my belly and felt it tumble!" I reply.
"My body is telling me it's time to eat!"

The teacher claps and grins. "That's wonderful because it's lunchtime!"

In the lunchroom, after I finish eating, I hear my tummy again—no more grumble rumbles! My belly is telling me I'm full, so I stop eating and clean up.

"I'm getting the hang of this" I think during art time.

The more I listen, the more I can hear my body talk to me. Just then, I feel a little pressure in my bottom and realize… my body is saying, "I have to poop!"

So I stop what I'm doing and head to the bathroom.

Later, my mouth feels dry, scratchy, and thirsty—like a desert! My body is talking, telling me to drink some water. I grab my bottle and take a big sip. Ahh!

On my way out of class, I bump my knee on the corner of a table.

"Ouch!" My knee starts to throb and thump. It's saying, "OW! Take a break! Ask for help!" So I go to the nurse to rest.

During recess, I run and play in the sun until my skin feels sweaty and warm. My body speaks again: "It's too hot out here!"

I find a shady spot under a tree and sit there, picking dandelions, until my body feels cool and calm again.

When I get home, I feel wiggly, jiggly, and full of energy.

My body is singing to me, saying, "Move, move, move!" So I dance around the room, jumping, twirling and shaking until I feel great.

After dinner, I have a nice warm bath, brush my teeth, and snuggle into bed with my favorite book. My body feels heavy, calm, and quiet.

My body is whispering now... "I'm sleepy."
I close my eyes, snuggle under the covers, and start to drift off to sleep.

As I lie in bed, I think about all the ways my body talks to me. Now that I'm listening, it feels like my body is my best friend! My body talks to me and helps me stay safe and happy—and I can always take a moment to stop and listen.

I am learning: how to listen to my body!

I am LEARNING

HOW TO LISTEN TO MY BODY

Resources for Caregivers

Interoception is our body's ability to sense internal signals. It helps us recognize and respond to physical sensations like hunger, thirst, needing the bathroom, or feeling pain

Children with challenges in interoception may have difficulty identifying and responding to these signals. They might not realize they're hungry until they're overly hungry or may misinterpret sensations, leading to confusion or distress.

For children, interoception plays a crucial role in identifying their needs, managing emotions, and feeling safe and secure in their environment.

Understanding and responding to interoception helps children:
- <u>Understand their needs:</u> Recognizing when they're hungry, thirsty, or need the bathroom and learning to respond to those needs.
- <u>Improve regulation:</u> Listening and responding to body cues gives the body a chance to feel regulated.
- <u>Feel safe and secure:</u> Consistently responding to bodily cues fosters trust in their ability to meet their needs, creating a foundation of safety and predictability.

Playful Games to Build Interoception Awareness

Body Detective
Play: Take turns describing a body sensation ("My stomach is growling") and guessing what it means (hunger).

Why: Builds connections between physical sensations and needs.

Body Scan
Play: Pretend you are a robot scanning your body systems for "bugs". Start at your head and go all the way to your toes checking in with each body part to see how it feels. does the throat need water? tummy need food?

Why: Builds awareness of body sensations

Body Cue Charades
Play: without using words act out a sensation such as hungry, hurt, or thirsty - have your partner guess the body cue

Why: helps build connections between how body cues might look and feel.

What's The Temp?
Play: Use items with different temperatures (e.g., a warm washcloth, ice cube). Have your child use their senses to describe the temperature.

Why: Increases awareness of temperature changes and how your body can sense temperature

www.ingramcontent.com/pod-product-compliance
Lightning Source LLC
Chambersburg PA
CBHW041437120626
46547CB00002B/251